The Greatest Thing in the World

The Greatest Thing in the World

in the World

Henry Drummond

Tole™

Morgantown, KY

The Greatest Thing in the World first published in 1884.

ISBN: 978-1-948696-55-5 (Paperback)

Cover: Created and licensed through Canva; Henry Drummond Ð Stock image © ilbusca

Printed in the United States of America

TOLE PUBLISHING, PO BOX 1098, MORGANTOWN, KY, 42261-8411
www.tolepublishing.com

Contents

Forward

I was staying with a party of friends in a country house during my visit to England in 1884. On Sunday evening as we sat around the fire, they asked me to read and expound some portion of Scripture. Being tired after the services of the day, I told them to ask Henry Drummond, who was one of the party. After some urging he drew a small Testament from his hip pocket, opened it at the 13th chapter of I Corinthians, and began to speak on the subject of Love.

It seemed to me that I had never heard anything so beautiful, and I determined not to rest until I brought Henry Drummond to Northfield to deliver that address. Since then I have requested the principals of my schools to have it read before the students every year. The one great need in our Christian life is love, more love to God and to each other. Would that we could all move into that Love chapter, and live there.

D. L. Moody.

1 Corinthians 13 (KJV, ESV)

King James Version (KJV)

[1] Though I speak with the tongues of men and of angels, and have not charity, I am become as sounding brass, or a tinkling cymbal.

[2] And though I have the gift of prophecy, and understand all mysteries, and all knowledge; and though I have all faith, so that I could remove mountains, and have not charity, I am nothing.

[3] And though I bestow all my goods to feed the poor, and though I give my body to be burned, and have not charity, it profiteth me nothing.

[4] Charity suffereth long, and is kind; charity

envieth not; charity vaunteth not itself, is not puffed up,

5 Doth not behave itself unseemly, seeketh not her own, is not easily provoked, thinketh no evil;

6 Rejoiceth not in iniquity, but rejoiceth in the truth;

7 Beareth all things, believeth all things, hopeth all things, endureth all things.

8 Charity never faileth: but whether there be prophecies, they shall fail; whether there be tongues, they shall cease; whether there be knowledge, it shall vanish away.

9 For we know in part, and we prophesy in part.

10 But when that which is perfect is come, then that which is in part shall be done away.

11 When I was a child, I spake as a child, I understood as a child, I thought as a child: but when I became a man, I put away childish things.

12 For now we see through a glass, darkly; but

then face to face: now I know in part; but then shall I know even as also I am known.

¹³ And now abideth faith, hope, charity, these three; but the greatest of these is charity.

English Standard Version (ESV)

¹ If I speak in the tongues of men and of angels, but have not love, I am a noisy gong or a clanging cymbal. ² And if I have prophetic powers, and understand all mysteries and all knowledge, and if I have all faith, so as to remove mountains, but have not love, I am nothing. ³ If I give away all I have, and if I deliver up my body to be burned, but have not love, I gain nothing.

⁴ Love is patient and kind; love does not envy or boast; it is not arrogant 5 or rude. It does not insist on its own way; it is not irritable or resentful; ⁶ it does not rejoice at wrongdoing, but rejoices with the truth. ⁷ Love bears all things, believes all things, hopes all things, endures all things.

⁸ Love never ends. As for prophecies, they will pass away; as for tongues, they will cease; as for

knowledge, it will pass away. [9] For we know in part and we prophesy in part, [10] but when the perfect comes, the partial will pass away. [11] When I was a child, I spoke like a child, I thought like a child, I reasoned like a child. When I became a man, I gave up childish ways. [12] For now we see in a mirror dimly, but then face to face. Now I know in part; then I shall know fully, even as I have been fully known.

[13] So now faith, hope, and love abide, these three; but the greatest of these is love.

1

Love: The Greatest Thing in the World

"Love is the highest, the pinnacle...Just as a rose in full bloom is greater than the stem that bears it, so, while faith is most needful, and hope most cheering, love is the most beautiful and brightest of the three." ~ Charles Spurgeon

Everyone has asked himself the great question of antiquity as of the modern world: What is the *summum bonum*—the supreme good? You have life before you. Once only you can live it. What is the noblest object of desire, the supreme gift to covet?

We have been accustomed to be told that the greatest thing in the religious world is faith. That great word has been the key-note for centuries of the popular religion, and we have easily learned to look upon it as the greatest thing in the world. Well, we are wrong. If we have been told that, we may miss the mark. In the thirteenth chapter of first Corinthians, Paul takes us to

CHRISTIANITY AT ITS SOURCE;

and there we see, *"The greatest of these is love."*

It is not an oversight. Paul was speaking of faith just a moment before. He says, *"If I have all faith, so that I can remove mountains, and have not love, I am nothing."* So far from forgetting, he deliberately contrasts them, *"Now abideth faith, hope, love,"* and without a moment's hesitation the decision falls, *"The greatest of these is love."*

And it is not prejudice. A man is apt to recommend to others his own strong point. Love was not Paul's strong point. The observing student can detect a beautiful tenderness growing and ripening all through his character as Paul gets old; but the hand that wrote, *"The greatest of these is love,"* when we meet it first, is stained with blood.

Nor is this letter to the Corinthians peculiar in singling out love as the *summum bonum.* The masterpieces of Christianity are agreed about it. Peter says, *"Above all things have fervent love among yourselves."* [1] Above all things. And John goes farther, *"God is love."* [2]

You remember the profound remark which Paul makes elsewhere, *"Love is the fulfilling of the law."* [3] Did you ever think what he meant by that? In those days men were working the passage to Heaven by keeping the Ten Commandments, and the hundred and ten other commandments which they had manufactured out of them. Christ came and basically said, "I will show you a more simple way. If you do one thing, you will do these hundred and ten things, without ever thinking about them. If

1. 1 Peter 4:8
2. 1 John 4:8, 16
3. Romans 13:10

you love, you will unconsciously fulfill the whole law."[4]

You can readily see for yourselves how that must be so. Take any of the commandments. *"Thou shalt have no other gods before Me."*[5] If a man loves God, you will not require to tell him that. Love is the fulfilling of that law. *"Take not His name in vain."*[6] Would he ever dream of taking His name in vain if he loved him? *"Remember the Sabbath day to keep it holy."*[7] Would he not be too glad to have one day in seven to dedicate more exclusively to the object of his affection? Love would fulfill all these laws regarding God.

And so, if he loved man, you would never think of telling him to honor his father and mother. He could not do anything else. It would be preposterous to tell him not to kill. You could only

4. "You shall love the Lord your God with all your heart and with all your soul and with all your mind. This is the great and first commandment. And a second is like it: You shall love your neighbor as yourself. On these two commandments depend all the Law and the Prophets." The Holy Bible: English Standard Version (Wheaton, IL: Crossway Bibles, 2016), Matthew 22:37–40.
5. Exodus 20:3; Deuteronomy 5:7
6. Exodus 20:7; Deuteronomy 5:11
7. Exodus 20:8

insult him if you suggested that he should not steal—how could he steal from those he loved? It would be superfluous to beg him not to bear false witness against his neighbor. If he loved him it would be the last thing he would do. And you would never dream of urging him not to covet what his neighbors had. He would rather they possessed it than himself. In this way *"Love is the fulfilling of the law."* It is the rule for fulfilling all rules, the new commandment for keeping all the old commandments, Christ's one

SECRET OF THE CHRISTIAN LIFE.

Now Paul has learned that, and in this noble eulogy he has given us the most wonderful and original account extant of the *summum bonum*. We may divide it into three parts. At the beginning of the short chapter we have *Love* contrasted; in the heart of it, we have *Love* analyzed; toward the end, we have *Love* defended as the supreme gift.

2

The Contrast

"If there be no love to God, and no love to man, the vital element is wanting. Whatever sound we make if the Word of God is not in us, it is a sound that has no meaning, conveys no heavenly meaning. "I am become as sounding brass, or a tinkling cymbal." What if any of us who bear witness for Christ with our tongues should be found to be no better than this?" ~ Charles Spurgeon

Paul begins by contrasting *love* with other things that men in those days thought much of. I shall not attempt to go over these things in detail. Their inferiority is already obvious.

He contrasts it with eloquence. And what a noble gift it is, the power of playing upon the souls and wills of men, and rousing them to lofty purposes and holy deeds! Paul says, *"If I speak with the tongues of men and of angels, and have not love, I am become sounding brass, or a tinkling cymbal."* We all know why. We have all felt the brazenness of words without emotion, the hollowness, the unaccountable unpersuasiveness, of eloquence behind which lies no love.

He contrasts it with prophecy.[1] He contrasts it with mysteries. He contrasts it with faith. He contrasts it with charity. Why is love greater than faith? Because the end is greater than the means. And why is it greater than charity? Because the whole is greater than the part.

Love is greater than faith, because the end is greater than the means. What is the use of having faith? It

1. "prophecy" is "...in NT, gift of expounding scripture, or of speaking and preaching, under the influence of the Holy Spirit" Henry George Liddell et al., A Greek-English Lexicon (Oxford: Clarendon Press, 1996), 1539.

is to connect the soul with God. And what is the object of connecting man with God? That he may become like God. But God is love. Hence faith, the means, is in order to love, the end. Love, therefore, obviously is greater than faith. *"If I have all faith, so as to remove mountains, but have not love, I am nothing."*

It is greater than charity, again, because the whole is greater than a part. Charity is only a little bit of love, one of the innumerable avenues of love, and there may even be, and there is, a great deal of charity without love. It is a very easy thing to toss a copper to a beggar on the street; it is generally an easier thing than not to do it. Yet love is just as often in the withholding. We purchase relief from the sympathetic feelings roused by the spectacle of misery, at the copper's cost. It is too cheap—too cheap for us, and often too dear for the beggar. If we really loved him we would either do more for him, or less. Hence, *"If I bestow all my goods to feed the poor, but have not love it profiteth me nothing."*

Then Paul contrasts it with sacrifice and

martyrdom: *"If I give my body to be burned, but have not love, it profiteth me nothing."* Missionaries can take nothing greater to the heathen world than the impress and reflection of the love of God upon their own character. That is the universal language. It will take them years to speak in Chinese, or in the dialects of India. From the day they land, that language of love, understood by all, will be pouring forth its unconscious eloquence.

It is the man who is the missionary, it is not his words. His character is his message. In the heart of Africa, among the Great Lakes, I have come across black men and women who remembered the only white man they ever saw before—David Livingstone; and as you cross his footsteps in that dark continent,

MEN'S FACES LIGHT UP

as they speak of the kind doctor who passed there years ago. They could not understand him, but they felt the love that beat in his heart. They knew that it was love, although he spoke no word.

Take into your sphere of labor, where you also mean to lay down your life, that simple charm, and your lifework must succeed. You can take nothing greater, you need take nothing less. You may take every accomplishment; you may be braced for every sacrifice; but if you give your body to be burned, and have not love, it will profit you, and the cause of Christ, nothing.

3

The Analysis

"No sooner is love born than she finds herself at war. Everything is against her, for the world is full of envy, hate, and ill-will. I would warn the most loving-hearted that they have entered upon a war for peace, a strife for love: they are born to hate hatred, and to contend against contention. As the lily among thorns, so is love among the sons of men." ~ Charles Spurgeon

After contrasting *love* with these things, Paul, in three verses, very short, gives us an amazing analysis of what this supreme thing is.

I ask you to look at it. It is a compound thing, he tells us. It is like light. As you have seen a man of science take a beam of light and pass it through a crystal prism, as you have seen it come out on the other side of the prism broken up into its component colors—red, and blue, and yellow, and violet, and orange, and all the colors of the rainbow—so Paul passes this thing, love, through the magnificent prism of his inspired intellect, and it comes out on the other side broken up into its elements.

In these few words, we have what one might call

THE SPECTRUM OF LOVE,

the analysis of love. Will you observe what its elements are? Will you notice that they have common names; that they are virtues which we hear about every day; that they are things which can be practised by every man in every place in life; and how, by a multitude of small things and ordinary virtues, the supreme thing, the *summum bonum*, is made up?

The Spectrum of Love has nine ingredients:

- *Patience* "Love suffereth long."

- *Kindness* "And is kind."

- *Generosity* "Love envieth not."

- *Humility* "Love vaunteth not itself, is not puffed up."

- *Courtesy* "Doth not behave itself unseemly."

- *Unselfishness* "Seeketh not its own."

- *Good temper* "Is not provoked."

- *Guilelessness* "Taketh not account of evil."

- *Sincerity* "Rejoiceth not in unrighteousness, but rejoiceth with the truth."

Patience; kindness; generosity; humility; courtesy; unselfishness; good temper; guilelessness; sincerity—these make up the supreme gift, the stature of the perfect man.

You will observe that all are in relation to men,

in relation to life, in relation to the known today and the near tomorrow, and not to the unknown eternity. We hear much of love to God; Christ spoke much of love to man. We make a great deal of peace with heaven; Christ made much of peace on earth. Religion is not a strange or added thing, but the inspiration of the secular life, the breathing of an eternal spirit through this temporal world. The supreme thing, in short, is not a thing at all, but the giving of a further finish to the multitudinous words and acts which make up the sum of every common day.

Patience. This is the normal attitude of love; love passive, love waiting to begin; not in a hurry; calm; ready to do its work when the summons comes, but meantime wearing the ornament of a meek and quiet spirit. Love suffers long; beareth all things; believeth all things; hopeth all things. For Love understands, and therefore waits.

Kindness. Love active. Have you ever noticed how much of Christ's life was spent in doing kind things—in merely doing kind things? Run over it with that in view, and you will find that He spent a great proportion of His time simply in making people happy, in

DOING GOOD TURNS

to people. There is only one thing greater than happiness in the world, and that is holiness; and it is not in our keeping; but what God has put in our power is the happiness of those about us, and that is largely to be secured by our being kind to them.

"The greatest thing," says some one, "a man can do for his Heavenly Father is to be kind to some of His other children." I wonder why it is that we are not all kinder than we are? How much the world needs it! How easily it is done! How instantaneously it acts! How infallibly it is remembered! How superabundantly it pays itself back—for there is no debtor in the world so honorable, so superbly honorable, as love. *"Love never faileth."* Love is success, love is happiness, love is life. "Love," I say with Browning, "is energy of life."

"For life, with all it yields of joy or woe
And hope and fear,

Is just our chance o' the prize of learning love,—
How love might be, hath been indeed, and is."

Where love is, God is. He that dwells in love dwells in God. God is love. Therefore love. Without distinction, without calculation, without procrastination, love. Lavish it upon the poor, where it is very easy; especially upon the rich, who often need it most; most of all upon our equals, where it is very difficult, and for whom perhaps we each do least of all. There is a difference between trying to please and giving pleasure. Give pleasure. Lose no chance of giving pleasure; for that is the ceaseless and anonymous triumph of a truly loving spirit. "I shall pass through this world but once. Any good thing, therefore, that I can do, or any kindness that I can show to any human being, let me do it now. Let me not defer it or neglect it, for I shall not pass this way again."

Generosity. "*Love envieth not.*" This is love in competition with others. Whenever you attempt a good work you will find other men doing the same kind of work, and probably doing it better. Envy them not. Envy is a feeling of ill-will to those who are in the same line as ourselves, a spirit of covetousness and detraction. How little Christian work even is protection against un-Christian feeling! That most despicable of all the unworthy moods which cloud a Christian's soul assuredly waits for us on the threshold of every work, unless we are fortified with this grace of magnanimity[1]. Only one thing truly need the Christian envy—the large, rich, generous soul which *"envieth not."*

And then, after having learned all that, you have to learn this further thing, *humility*—to put a seal upon your lips and forget what you have done. After you have been kind, after love has stolen forth into the world and done its beautiful work, go back into the shade again and say nothing about it. Love hides even from itself. Love waives even self-satisfaction. *"Love vaunteth not itself, is not puffed up."* Humility—love hiding.

The fifth ingredient is a somewhat strange one to find in this *summum bonum*: *Courtesy.* This is love

---

1. "magnanimity" is "loftiness of spirit enabling one to bear trouble calmly, to disdain meanness and pettiness, and to display a noble generosity" Inc Merriam-Webster, Merriam-Webster's Collegiate Dictionary. (Springfield, MA: Merriam-Webster, Inc., 2003).

in society, love in relation to etiquette. *"Love does not behave itself unseemly."*

Politeness has been defined as love in trifles. Courtesy is said to be love in little things. And the one secret of politeness is to love.

Love cannot behave itself unseemly[2]. You can put the most untutored persons into the highest society, and if they have a reservoir of love in their heart they will not behave themselves unseemly. They simply cannot do it. Carlisle said of Robert Burns that there was no truer gentleman in Europe than the ploughman-poet. It was because he loved everything—the mouse, and the daisy, and all the things, great and small, that God had made. So with this simple passport he could mingle with any society, and enter courts and palaces from his little cottage on the banks of the Ayr.

You know the meaning of the word "gentleman." It means a gentle man—a man who does things gently, with love. That is the whole art and mystery of it. The gentle man cannot in the nature of things

2. KJV version reads "unseemly" where as the ESV reads "rude"

do an ungentle, an ungentlemanly thing. The ungentle soul, the inconsiderate, unsympathetic nature, cannot do anything else. *"Love doth not behave itself unseemly."*

Unselfishness. *"Love seeketh not her own."* Observe: Seeketh not even that which is her own. In Britain the Englishman is devoted, and rightly, to his rights. But there come times when a man may exercise even

THE HIGHER RIGHT

of giving up his rights.

Yet Paul does not summon us to give up our rights. Love strikes much deeper. It would have us not seek them at all, ignore them, eliminate the personal element altogether from our calculations.

It is not hard to give up our rights. They are often eternal. The difficult thing is to give up ourselves. The more difficult thing still is not to seek things for ourselves at all. After we have sought them, bought them, won them, deserved them, we have taken the cream off them for ourselves already.

Little cross then to give them up. But not to seek them, to look every man not on his own things, but on the things of others—that is the difficulty. *"Seekest thou great things for thyself?"* said the prophet; *"seek them not."*[3] Why? Because there is no greatness in things. Things cannot be great. The only greatness is unselfish love. Even self-denial in itself is nothing, is almost a mistake. Only a great purpose or a mightier love can justify the waste.

It is more difficult, I have said, not to seek our own at all than, having sought it, to give it up. I must take that back. It is only true of a partly selfish heart. Nothing is a hardship to love, and nothing is hard. I believe that Christ's *"yoke"*[4] is easy. Christ's yoke is just His way of taking life. And I believe it is an easier way than any other. I believe it is a happier way than any other. The most obvious lesson in Christ's teaching is that there is no happiness in having and getting anything, but

3. Jeremiah 45:5
4. "Come to me, all who labor and are heavy laden, and I will give you rest. Take my yoke upon you, and learn from me, for I am gentle and lowly in heart, and you will find rest for your souls. For my yoke is easy, and my burden is light." The Holy Bible: English Standard Version (Wheaton, IL: Crossway Bibles, 2016), Matthew 11:28–30.

only in giving. I repeat, there is no happiness in having or in getting, but only in giving. Half the world is on the wrong scent in pursuit of happiness. They think it consists in having and getting, and in being served by others. It consists in giving, and in serving others. *"He that would be great among you,"* said Christ, *"let him serve."*[5] He that would be happy, let him remember that there is but one way—*"it is more blessed, it is more happy, to give than to receive."*[6]

The next ingredient is a very remarkable one: *Good temper. "Love is not provoked."*

Nothing could be more striking than to find this here. We are inclined to look upon bad temper as a very harmless weakness. We speak of it as a mere infirmity of nature, a family failing, a matter of temperament, not a thing to take into very serious account in estimating a man's character. And yet here, right in the heart of this analysis of love, it finds a place; and the Bible again and again returns to condemn it as one of the most destructive elements in human nature.

5. Matthew 20:26
6. Acts 20:35

The peculiarity of ill temper is that it is the vice of the *virtuous*. It is often the one blot on an otherwise noble character. You know men who are all but *perfect* and women who would be *entirely perfect*, but for an easily ruffled, quick-tempered, or "touchy" disposition. This compatibility of ill temper with high moral character is one of the strangest and saddest problems of ethics. The truth is, there are two great classes of sins—sins of the body and sins of the disposition. The prodigal son may be taken as a type of the first, the elder brother of the second[7]. Now, society has no doubt whatever as to which of these is the worse. Its brand falls, without a challenge, upon the prodigal. But are we right? We have no balance to weigh one another's sins, and coarser and finer are but human words; but faults in the higher nature may be less venal than those in the lower, and to the eye of God, who is love, a sin against love may seem a hundred times more base. No form of vice, not worldliness, not greed of gold, not drunkenness itself, does more to un-Christianize society than evil temper. For embittering life, for breaking up

7. The Parable of the Lost Son-Luke 15:11-32

communities, for destroying the most sacred relationships, for devastating homes, for withering up men and women, for taking the bloom of childhood, in short,

FOR SHEER GRATUITOUS MISERY-PRODUCING POWER

this influence stands alone.

Look at the elder brother—moral, hard-working, patient, dutiful—let him get all credit for his virtues—look at this man, this baby, sulking outside his own father's door. *"He was angry,"* we read, *"and would not go in."*[8] Look at the effect upon the father, upon the servants, upon the happiness of the guests. Judge of the effect upon the prodigal—and how many prodigals are kept out of the kingdom of God by the unlovely character of those who profess to be inside. Analyze, as a study in temper, the thunder-cloud itself as it gathers upon the elder brother's brow. What is it made of? We find jealousy, anger, pride, uncharity, cruelty, self-righteousness, touchiness, doggedness,

8. Luke 15:28

sullenness—these are the ingredients of this dark and loveless soul. In varying proportions, also, these are the ingredients of all ill temper. Judge if such sins of the disposition are not worse to live in, and for others to live with, than the sins of the body. Did Christ indeed not answer the question Himself when He said, *"I say unto you that the publicans and the harlots go into the kingdom of heaven before you"*?[9] There is really no place in heaven for a disposition like this. A man with such a mood could only make Heaven miserable for all the people in it. Except, therefore, such a man be

BORN AGAIN,

he cannot, simply cannot, enter the kingdom of Heaven[10].

You will see then why temper is significant. It is not in what it is alone, but in what it reveals. This is why I speak of it with such unusual plainness. It is a test for love, a symptom, a revelation of an

9. Matthew 21:31
10. "Truly, truly, I say to you, unless one is born of water and the Spirit, he cannot enter the kingdom of God." The Holy Bible: English Standard Version (Wheaton, IL: Crossway Bibles, 2016), John 3:5.

unloving nature at bottom. It is the intermittent fever which bespeaks unintermittent disease within; the occasional bubble escaping to the surface which betrays some rottenness underneath; a sample of the most hidden products of the soul dropped involuntarily when off one's guard; in a word, the lightning form of a hundred hideous and un-Christian sins. A want of patience, a want of kindness, a want of generosity, a want of courtesy, a want of unselfishness, are all instantaneously symbolized in one flash of temper.

Hence it is not enough to deal with the temper. We must go to the source, and change the inmost nature, and the angry humors will die away of themselves. Souls are made sweet not by taking the acid fluids out, but by putting something in—a great love, a new Spirit, the Spirit of Christ. Christ, the Spirit of Christ, interpenetrating ours, sweetens, purifies, transforms all. This only can eradicate what is wrong, work a chemical change, renovate and regenerate, and rehabilitate the inner man. Will-power does not change men. Time does not change men.

CHRIST DOES.

Therefore, *"Let that mind be in you which was also in Christ Jesus."*[11]

Some of us have not much time to lose. Remember, once more, that this is a matter of life or death. I cannot help speaking urgently, for myself, for yourselves. *"Whoso shall offend one of these little ones, which* believe *in me, it were better for him that a millstone* were *hanged about his neck, and that he* were *drowned in the depth of the* sea."[12] That is to say, it is the deliberate verdict of the Lord Jesus that it is better not to live than not to love. It is better not to live than not to love.

Guilelessness and sincerity may be dismissed almost without a word. *Guilelessness* is the grace for suspicious people. The possession of it is

THE GREAT SECRET OF PERSONAL INFLUENCE.

You will find, if you think for a moment, that the

11. Philippians 2:5
12. Matthew 18:6; Mark 9:42

people who influence you are people who believe in you. In an atmosphere of suspicion men shrivel up; but in that atmosphere, they expand, and find encouragement and educative fellowship.

It is a wonderful thing that here and there in this hard, uncharitable world there should still be left a few rare souls who think no evil. This is the great unworldliness. Love *"thinketh no evil,"* imputes no motive, sees the bright side, puts the best construction on every action. What a delightful state of mind to live in! What a stimulus and benediction even to meet with it for a day! To be trusted is to be saved. And if we try to influence or elevate others, we shall soon see that success is in proportion to their belief of our belief in them. The respect of another is the first restoration of the self-respect a man has lost; our ideal of what he is becomes to him the hope and pattern of what he may become.

"Love rejoiceth not in unrighteousness, but rejoiceth with the truth." I have called this *Sincerity* from the words rendered in the Authorized Version by *"rejoiceth in the truth."* And, certainly, were this the

real translation, nothing could be more just; for he who loves will love truth not less than men. He will rejoice in the truth—rejoice not in what he has been taught to believe; not in this church's doctrine or in that; not in this *ism* or in that *ism*; but *"in the truth."* He will accept only what is real; he will strive to get at facts; he will search for truth with a humble and unbiased mind, and cherish whatever he finds at any sacrifice. But the more literal translation of the Revised Version calls for just such a sacrifice for truth's sake here. For what Paul really meant is, as we there read, *"Rejoiceth not in unrighteousness, but rejoiceth with the truth,"* a quality which probably no one English word—and certainly not "sincerity"—adequately defines. It includes, perhaps more strictly, the self-restraint which refuses to make capital out of others' faults; the charity which delights not in exposing the weakness of others, but *"covereth all things"*; the sincerity of purpose which endeavors to see things as they are, and rejoices to find them better than suspicion feared or calumny denounced.

So much for the analysis of love. Now the business

of our lives is to have these things fitted into our characters. That is the supreme work to which we need to address ourselves in this world, to learn love. Is life not full of opportunities for learning love? Every man and woman every day has a thousand of them. The world is not a playground; it is a schoolroom. Life is not a holiday, but an education. And

THE ONE ETERNAL LESSON

for us all is how better we can love.

What makes a man a good cricketer? Practice. What makes a man a good artist, a good sculptor, a good musician? Practice. What makes a man a good linguist, a good stenographer? Practice. What makes a man a good man? Practice. Nothing else. There is nothing capricious about religion. We do not get the soul in different ways, under different laws, from those in which we get the body and the mind. If a man does not exercise his arm he develops no biceps muscle; and if a man does not exercise his soul, he acquires no muscle in his soul, no strength of character, no vigor of moral fibre, no beauty of spiritual growth. Love is not a thing of enthusiastic emotion. It is a rich, strong, manly, vigorous expression of the whole round Christian character—the Christlike nature in its fullest development. And the constituents of this great character are only to be built up by

CEASELESS PRACTICE.

What was Christ doing in the carpenter's shop? Practising. Though perfect, we read that He learned obedience, and grew in wisdom and in favor with God.[13] Do not quarrel, therefore, with your lot in life. Do not complain of its never-ceasing cares, its petty environment, the vexations you have to stand, the small and sordid souls you have to live and work with. Above all, do not resent temptation; do not be perplexed because it seems to thicken round you more and more, and ceases neither for effort nor for agony nor prayer. That is your practice. That is the practice which God appoints you; and it is having its work in making you patient, and humble, and generous, and unselfish, and kind, and courteous. Do not

13. Luke 2:52

grudge the hand that is moulding the still too shapeless image within you. It is growing more beautiful, though you see it not; and every touch of temptation may add to its perfection. Therefore keep in the midst of life. Do not isolate yourself. Be among men and among things, and among troubles, and difficulties, and obstacles. You remember Goethe's words: "Talent develops itself in solitude; character in the stream of life." Talent develops itself in solitude—the talent of prayer, of faith, of meditation, of seeing the unseen; character grows in the stream of the world's life. That chiefly is where men are to learn love.

How? Now, how? To make it easier, I have named a few of the elements of love. But these are only elements. Love itself can never be defined. Light is something more than the sum of its ingredients—a glowing, dazzling, tremulous ether. And love is something more than all its elements—a palpitating, quivering, sensitive, living thing. By synthesis of all the colors, men can make whiteness, they cannot make light. By synthesis of all the virtues, men can make virtue, they cannot make love. How then are we to have this transcendent living whole conveyed into our souls? We brace our wills to secure it. We try to copy those who have it. We lay down rules about it. We watch. We pray. But these things alone will not bring love into our nature. Love is an effect. And only as we fulfill the right condition can we have the effect produced. Shall I tell you what the cause is?

If you turn to the Revised Version of the First Epistle of John you find these words: *"We love because He first loved us."*[14] *"We love,"* not *"We love Him."* That is the way the old version has it, and it is quite wrong. *"We love—because He first loved us."* Look at that word *"because."* It is the cause of which I have spoken. *"Because He first loved us,"* the effect follows that we love, we love Him, we love all men. We cannot help it. Because He loved us, we love, we love everybody. Our heart is slowly changed. Contemplate the love of Christ, and you will love. Stand before that mirror, reflect Christ's character, and you will be changed into the same image from tenderness to tenderness. There is no

14. 1 John 4:19

other way. You cannot love to order. You can only look at the lovely object, and fall in love with it, and grow into likeness to it. And so look at Christ's perfect character, His perfect life. Look at

THE GREAT SACRIFICE

as He laid down Himself, all through life, and upon the cross of Calvary; and you must love Him. And loving Him, you must become like Him. Love begets love. It is a process of induction. Put a piece of iron in the presence of an electrified body, and that piece of iron for a time becomes electrified. It is changed into a temporary magnet in the mere presence of a permanent magnet, and as long as you leave the two side by side, they are both magnets alike. Remain side by side with Him who loved us, and

GAVE HIMSELF FOR US,

and you, too, will become a permanent magnet, a permanently attractive force; and like Him you will draw all men unto you, like Him you will be drawn unto all men. That is the inevitable effect of divine love. Any man who fulfills that cause must have that effect produced in him.

Try to give up the idea that religion comes to us by chance, or by mystery, or by caprice. It comes to us by natural law, or by supernatural law, for all law is divine.

Edward Irving went to see a dying boy once, and when he entered the room he just put his hand on the sufferer's head, and said, "My boy, God loves you," and went away. The boy started from his bed, and called out to the people in the house,

"God loves me! God loves me!"

One word! It changed that boy. The sense that God loved him overpowered him, melted him down, and began the creating of a new heart in him. And that is how the love of God melts down the unlovely heart in man, and begets in him the new creature, who is patient and humble and gentle and unselfish. And there is no other way to get it. There is no mystery about it. We love others, we love everybody, we love our enemies, because He first loved us.

4

The Defense

**"Much of what we call knowledge, much of what
we call eloquence, will all be put away. As our
spiritual growth shall increase, we shall not
want these childish things." ~ Charles Spurgeon**

Now I have a closing sentence or two to add about
Paul's reason for singling out love as the supreme
possession.

It is a very remarkable reason. In a single word
it is this: it lasts. *"Love,"* urges Paul, *"never faileth."*
Then he begins again one of his marvelous lists of
the great things of the day, and exposes them one

by one. He runs over the things that men thought were going to last, and shows that they are all fleeting, temporary, passing away.

"Whether there be prophecies, they shall be done away." It was the mother's ambition for her boy in those days that he should become a prophet. For hundreds of years God had never spoken by means of any prophet, and at that time the prophet was greater than the king. Men waited wistfully for another messenger to come, and hung upon his lips when he appeared, as upon the very voice of God. Paul says, *"Whether there be prophecies, they shall fail."* The Bible is full of prophecies. One by one they have *"failed"*; that is, having been fulfilled, their work is finished; they have nothing more to do now in the world except to feed a devout man's faith.

Then Paul talks about tongues. That was another thing that was greatly coveted. *"Whether there be tongues, they shall cease."* As we all know, many many centuries have passed since tongues have been known in this world. They have ceased. Take it in any sense you like. Take it, for illustration merely, as languages in general—a sense which was not in Paul's mind at all, and which though it cannot give us the specific lesson, will point the general truth. Consider the words in which these chapters were written—Greek. It has gone. Take the Latin—the other great tongue of those days. It ceased long ago. Look at the Indian language. It is ceasing. The language of Wales, of Ireland, of the Scottish Highlands, is dying before our eyes. The most popular book in the English tongue at the present time, except the Bible, is one of Dickens' works, his Pickwick Papers. It is largely written in the language of London street-life, and experts assure us that in fifty years it will be unintelligible to the average English reader.

Then Paul goes farther, and with even greater boldness adds, *"Whether there be knowledge, it shall be done away."* The wisdom of the ancients, where is it? It is wholly gone. A schoolboy today knows more than Sir Isaac Newton knew; his knowledge has vanished away. You put yesterday's newspaper in the fire: its knowledge has vanished away. You buy the old editions of the great encyclopædias for a few cents: their knowledge has vanished away. Look how the coach has been superseded by the use of steam. Look how electricity has superseded that, and swept a hundred almost new inventions into oblivion. One of the greatest living authorities, Sir William Thompson, said in Scotland, at a meeting at which I was present, "The steam-engine is passing away." *"Whether there be knowledge, it shall vanish away."* At every workshop you will see, in the back yard, a heap of old iron, a few wheels, a few levers, a few cranks, broken and eaten with rust. Twenty years ago that was the pride of the city. Men flocked in from the country to see the great invention; now it is superseded, its day is done. And all the boasted science and philosophy of this day will soon be old.

In my time at the University of Edinburgh, the greatest figure in the faculty was Sir James Simpson, the discoverer of chloroform. Recently his successor and nephew, Professor Simpson, was asked by the librarian of the University to go to the library and pick out the books on his subject (midwifery) that were no longer needed. His reply to the librarian was this:

> "Take every textbook that is more than ten years old and put it down in the cellar."

Sir James Simpson was a great authority only a few years ago: men came from all parts of the earth to consult him, and almost the whole teaching of that time is consigned by the science of today to oblivion. And in every branch of science, it is the same. *"Now we know in part. We see through a glass darkly."* Knowledge does not last.

Can you tell me anything that is going to last? Many things Paul did not condescend to name. He did not mention money, fortune, fame; but he picked out the great things of his time, the things the best men thought had something in them, and brushed them masterfully aside. Paul had no charge against these things in themselves. All he said about them was that they would not last. They were great things, but not supreme things. There were things beyond them. What we are stretches past what we do, beyond what we possess. Many things that men denounce as sins are not sins; but they are temporary. And that is a favorite argument of the New Testament. John says of the world, not that it is wrong, but simply that it *"passeth away."* There is a great deal in the world that is delightful and beautiful; there is a great deal in it that is great and engrossing; but

IT WILL NOT LAST.

All that is in the world, the lust of the eye, the lust of the flesh, and the pride of life, are but for a little while. Love not the world therefore. Nothing that it contains is worth the life and consecration of an immortal soul. The immortal soul must give itself to something that is immortal. And the only immortal things are these: *"Now abideth faith, hope, love, but the greatest of these is love."*

Some think the time may come when two of these three things will also pass away—faith into sight, hope into fruition. Paul does not say so. We know but little now about the conditions of the life that is to come. But what is certain is that love must last. God, the eternal God, is love. Covet, therefore, that everlasting gift, that one thing which it is certain is going to stand, that one coinage which will be current in the universe when all the other coinages of all the nations of the world shall be useless and unhonored. You will give yourselves to many things, give yourself first to divine love. Hold things in their proportion. Let at least the first great object of our lives be to achieve the character defended in these words, the character—and it is the character of Christ—which is built around love.

I have said this thing is eternal. Did you ever notice how continually John associates love and faith with eternal life? I was not told when I was a boy that *"God so loved the world that He gave His only-begotten Son, that whosoever believeth in Him should have everlasting life."*[1] What I was told, I remember, was, that God so loved the world that, if I trusted in Him, I was to have a thing called peace, or I was to have rest, or I was to have joy, or I was to have safety. But I had to find out for myself that whosoever trusteth in Him—that is, whosoever

1. John 3:16

loveth Him, for trust is only the avenue to love—hath

EVERLASTING LIFE.

The gospel offers a man a life. Never offer a man a thimbleful of gospel. Do not offer them merely joy, or merely peace, or merely rest, or merely safety; tell them how Christ came to give men a more abundant life than they have, a life abundant in love, and therefore abundant in salvation for themselves, and large in enterprise for the alleviation and redemption of the world. Then only can the gospel take hold of the whole of a man, body, soul and spirit, and give to each part of his nature its exercise and reward. Many of the current so-called gospels are addressed only to a part of man's nature. They offer peace, not life; faith, not love; justification, not regeneration. And men slip back again from such religion because it has never really held them. Their nature was not all in it. It offered no deeper and gladder life-current than the life that was lived before. Surely it stands to reason that only a fuller love can compete with the love of the world.

To love abundantly is to live abundantly, and to love forever is to live forever. Hence, eternal life is inextricably bound up with love. We want to live forever for the same reason that we want to live tomorrow. Why do we want to live tomorrow? Is it because there is someone who loves you, and whom you want to see tomorrow, and be with, and love back? There is no other reason why we should live on than that we love and are beloved. It is when a man has no one to love him that he commits suicide. So long as he has friends, those who love him and whom he loves, he will live, because to live is to love. Be it but the love of a dog, it will keep him in life; but let that go, he has no contact with life, no reason to live. He dies by his own hand.

Eternal life also is to know God, and God is love. This is Christ's own definition. Ponder it. *"This is life eternal, that they might know Thee the only true God, and Jesus Christ whom Thou hast sent."*[2] Love must be eternal. It is what God is. On the last analysis, then, love is life. Love never faileth, and

2. John 17:3

life never faileth, so long as there is love. That is the philosophy of what Paul is showing us; the reason why in the nature of things love should be the supreme thing—because it is going to last; because in the nature of things it is eternal life. It is a thing that we are living now, not that we get when we die; that we shall have a poor chance of getting when we die unless we are living now.

NO WORSE FATE

can befall a man in this world than to live and grow old alone, unloving and unloved. To be lost is to live in an unregenerate condition, loveless and unloved; and to be saved is to love, and he that dwelleth in love dwelleth already in God. For God is love.

Now I have all but finished. How many of you will join me in reading this chapter once a week for the next three months? A man did that once and it changed his whole life. Will you do it? It is for the greatest thing in the world. You might begin by reading it every day, especially the verses which describe the perfect character. *"Love suffereth long, and is kind; love envieth not; love vaunteth not itself."* Get these ingredients into your life. Then everything that you do is eternal. It is worth doing. It is worth giving time to. No man can become a saint in his sleep; and to fulfill the condition required demands a certain amount of prayer and meditation and time, just as improvement in any direction, bodily or mental, requires preparation and care. Address yourselves to that one thing; at any cost have this transcendent character exchanged for yours.

You will find as you look back upon your life that the moments that stand out, the moments when you have really lived, are the moments when you have done things in a spirit of love. As memory scans the past, above and beyond all the transitory pleasures of life, there leap forward those supreme hours when you have been enabled to do unnoticed kindnesses to those round about you, things too trifling to speak about, but which you feel have entered into your eternal life. I have seen almost all the beautiful things God has made; I have enjoyed almost every pleasure that He has planned for man;

and yet as I look back I see standing out above all the life that has gone four or five short experiences, when the love of God reflected itself in some poor imitation, some small act of love of mine, and these seem to be the things which alone of all one's life abide. Everything else in all our lives is transitory. Every other good is visionary. But the acts of love which no man knows about, or can ever know about—they never fail.

In the Gospel of Matthew, where The Judgment Day is depicted for us in the imagery of One seated upon a throne and dividing the sheep from the goats[3], the test of a man then is not, "How have I believed?" but "How have I loved?" The test of religion, the final test of religion, is not religiousness, but love. I say the final test of religion at that great day is not religiousness, but love; not what I have done, not what I have believed, not what I have achieved, but how I have discharged the common charities of life. Sins of commission in that awful indictment are not even referred to. By what we have not done, by sins of omission,

3. Matthew 25:31-46

we are judged. It could not be otherwise. For the withholding of love is the negation of the spirit of Christ, the proof that we never knew Him, that for us He lived in vain. It means that He suggested nothing in all our thoughts, that He inspired nothing in all our lives, that we were not once near enough to Him, to be seized with the spell of His compassion for the world. It means that—

"I lived for myself, I thought for myself,
For myself, and none beside—
Just as if Jesus had never lived,
As if He had never died."

Thank God the Christianity of today is coming nearer the world's need. Live to help that on. Thank God men know better, by a hair's breadth, what religion is, what God is, who Christ is, where Christ is. Who is Christ? He who fed the hungry, clothed the naked, visited the sick. And where is Christ? Where?—*"Whoso shall receive a little child in My name receiveth Me."*[4] And who are Christ's? *"Every one that loveth is born of God."*[5]

4. Luke 9:48
5. 1 John 4:7